THOSE CLOUDS SURE LOOK FLUFFY!

WEATHER BOOKS GRADE 4

CHILDREN'S EARTH SCIENCE BOOKS

BABY PROFESSOR

EDUCATION KIDS

Speedy Publishing LLC
40 E. Main St. #1156
Newark, DE 19711
www.speedypublishing.com
Copyright 2017

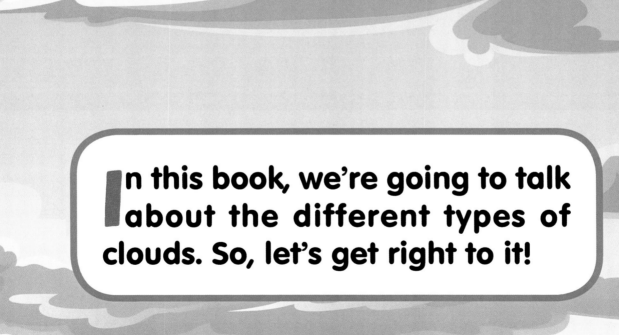

In this book, we're going to talk about the different types of clouds. So, let's get right to it!

Most days, when you look up into the sky, you see clouds floating by. The clouds are different shapes and sometimes you can tell by looking at them what kind of weather it's going to be. Certain types of clouds are white and fluffy. They look like floating cotton balls in the sky. Others look more like streaks. At times, they block the light from the sun and the sky gets darker.

The shapes of clouds are very interesting. Sometimes they look like animals, such as a bunny or a bear or maybe even a giraffe. It's easy to daydream when you're watching clouds. If you daydream a lot, your teacher might say that you have your "head in the clouds." Daydreamers aren't the only ones who like clouds.

Meteorologists study clouds to learn more about the weather. They research the composition of clouds so they can predict the weather better.

WHAT IS A CLOUD MADE OF?

Clouds are made up of moisture. They are either made of tiny water droplets or small particles of frozen water in the form of crystals.

HOW DOES THE ATMOSPHERE FORM A CLOUD?

All of the air in our atmosphere contains a percentage of water vapor. Warm air can contain more of this vapor than cold air can. As warm air travels upward, it cools.

WATER VAPOR

CLOUDS

The water vapor that the warm air contains changes into small droplets of either water or small particles of ice. As the air continues to cool, more and more droplets form, and soon they create what we see as a cloud.

WHY ARE SOME CLOUDS WHITE?

If you've ever seen the rainbow effect from a prism, then you know that each color has its own special wavelength. The water droplets or crystals of ice that form the clouds are of sufficient size to scatter the light. The seven wavelengths of violet, indigo, blue, green, yellow, orange, and red join together to produce white.

RAINBOW

GREY CLOUDS IN SKY

WHY DO CLOUDS CHANGE TO GRAY?

The water droplets and ice crystals in a cloud scatter the light, which makes the clouds look white. However, if the clouds change and get thicker or higher in the sky, not all the light gets through, which gives the clouds a gray or dark appearance. Sometimes other clouds block the sun from getting through, which darkens the clouds as well.

THE LEVELS OF CLOUDS

If you look up at the sky, you can see why meteorologists and scientists would use levels to describe clouds. Some clouds are positioned very high in the sky. Others are mid-range and still others are low-level clouds that are closer to the Earth's surface. There are ten distinct types of clouds and they have been categorized depending on the level of the sky where they form.

CLOUD ON HIGH LEVEL

HIGH-LEVEL CLOUDS

Clouds that form at a level about 20,000 feet from the Earth's surface are high-level clouds. It's colder up there in this part of the atmosphere, so these clouds are composed of crystals of ice. The names of the clouds that are described as high-level have either "cirro" or "cirrus" in their prefixes. The word "cirrus" comes from the Latin word that describes a lock of hair. This description fits them because they are often wispy-looking.

MIDDLE-LEVEL CLOUDS

Clouds that float in the middle-level of the atmosphere form at the range of 6,500 feet to 20,000 feet from Earth's surface. Some of these clouds are made of droplets of water while others are composed of crystals of ice. These clouds usually have the word "alto" as part of their names. In Latin, the word "alto" means "high" or "elevated."

LOW LEVEL CLOUDS

LOW-LEVEL CLOUDS

Clouds that float below 6,500 feet in the sky are described as low-level clouds. The air is warmer at this level so they are primarily composed of water droplets. The names for these clouds include the word "stratus," which comes from the Latin word that means "layers."

VERTICAL CLOUDS

Some clouds stretch vertically in the sky through more than one level. The names for these clouds include the word "cumulus." The word "cumulus" comes from a Latin word that means "heap" or "pile."

NAMES FOR THE
TYPES OF CLOUDS

HIGH-LEVEL

CIRRUS

Cirrus clouds are thin and kind of wispy looking like strands of hair. These clouds show up on good weather days at the higher level of the sky.

CIRROCUMULUS

Cirrocumulus clouds look like balls of cotton that have been grouped together in the higher level of the sky.

CIRROSTRATUS

Usually these flat clouds appear on overcast days at the higher level of the sky. Meteorologists know that cirrostratus clouds typically signal that rain is coming.

MIDDLE-LEVEL

ALTOSTRATUS

When these gray clouds cover the middle portion of the sky, it usually means rain is coming. Altostratus clouds only let a little bit of sunlight through.

ALTOCUMULUS

Altocumulus clouds are rather small. They are generally white as well as puffy and they float at the middle level of the sky.

NIMBOSTRATUS

Nimbostratus clouds are thick and dark gray in color. They appear in the middle level or low level of the sky. They pour out rain or sometimes snow.

LOW-LEVEL

STRATUS

Stratus clouds float at the lower level of the sky. They are rather flat and when they show up they sometimes cover a good portion of the sky. They are gray and usually produce a very light rain or a drizzle.

STRATOCUMULUS

Sometimes stratocumulus clouds can change into nimbostratus clouds. They frequently produce a little bit of rain and look gray and puffy as they float at the lower level of the sky.

VERTICAL

CUMULUS

Cumulus clouds span the lower level to the middle level of the sky. These are the clouds we think of when we imagine huge, bright-white, puffy clouds. Cumulus clouds are quite beautiful and sometimes look like different, interesting shapes. Usually, we see these clouds during good weather, however, they sometimes turn into cumulonimbus clouds.

CUMULONIMBUS

   Cumulonimbus clouds span from the low level of the sky to the high level. They can be scary because they cause large, dramatic thunderstorms resulting in heavy rain or hail. Sometimes they even cause tornadoes!

°C

°F

50

120

40

100

TEMPERATURE

WHY DO CLOUDS FORM AT DIFFERENT HEIGHTS?

The quantity of water vapor, the temperature at different points in the atmosphere, the speed of the wind, and the interaction of masses of air all have an effect on why clouds form at the different levels of the atmosphere.

HOW DO CLOUDS FLOAT?

You may be wondering how clouds float in the air since they are composed of water. The tiny drops of water have quite a bit of surface area and this helps prevent them from falling, just like a speck of dust that you see floating in the air. Even though these droplets are small and very lightweight, they would fall down eventually if the warm air didn't continue to rise underneath them. The warm air rises and cools. This process is what forms clouds and keeps them floating in the atmosphere.

THE UNUSUAL TYPES OF CLOUDS

MAMMATUS

Mammatus clouds look like bulges. They hang from the bottom of cumulonimbus clouds and they usually signal some type of weather disturbance.

LENTICULAR

The wind around mountains sometimes produces some interesting cloud effects. Lenticular clouds are caused by these winds. They look like white flying saucers poised over the mountaintops.

GREEN

If you see green or yellowish clouds, it might be good to take cover. Although meteorologists don't know the exact reason for the greenish cast, it's caused by the high amount of liquid and hail saturation inside these clouds. These clouds are frequently seen over the Great Plains. They are connected with hail and sometimes tornadoes.

FRACTUS

Fractus clouds are ragged fragments of clouds. They have been broken off a larger cloud by the force of powerful winds. They look something like pieces of cotton candy that have been shredded in irregular shapes.

FASCINATING FACTS ABOUT CLOUDS

- Sometimes jets form clouds in the sky. These types of clouds are known as contrails.

- A cloud that forms at or near the Earth's surface is known as fog.

- Cirrus clouds that travel in the higher-level sky sometimes move at a rate of up to 100 miles per hour.

AN AIRPLANE FLYING HIGH IN THE SKY LEAVES CONTRAILS

- Earth is not the only planet in our solar system that has clouds. The planet Venus as well as the planets Jupiter and Saturn also have clouds in their atmospheres.

- One cumulus cloud can actually have a weight of hundreds of tons even though it floats!

- Thunderstorm clouds usually travel around 30-40 miles per hour.

The next time your teacher says you have "your head in the clouds," you should be able to tell him or her which clouds they are!

Awesome! Now you know more about clouds and the weather. You can find more Earth Science books from Baby Professor by searching the website of your favorite book retailer.

Visit

BABY PROFESSOR
EDUCATION KIDS

www.BabyProfessorBooks.com

to download Free Baby Professor eBooks and view
our catalog of new and exciting Children's Books

Made in the USA
Las Vegas, NV
26 March 2021